THE UNTRUTH OF KINDNESS

HOW AVOIDING DISCOMFORT STIFLES GROWTH

A.E. HOWLAND

Copyright © *A.E. Howland,* 2025
All Rights Reserved

This book is subject to the condition that no part of this book is to be reproduced, transmitted in any form or means; electronic or mechanical, stored in a retrieval system, photocopied, recorded, scanned, or otherwise. Any of these actions require the proper written permission of the author.

Table of Content

Introduction 14

    The UnTruth of Kindness 14

    The True Cost of Avoidance 15

    Embracing Brutal Honesty 16

Chapter 1 Defining UnTruth 1

    What is UnTruth? 1

    The True Meaning of Brutal Honesty 2

    The Pitfalls of Avoidance 2

    Honesty as a Growth Catalyst 4

    Reflection Prompts 6

    Challenge: Speak an Uncomfortable Truth 8

    Sources for Chapter 1 8

    Notes Section 9

Chapter 2 Growth Through Discomfort 10

    Why Discomfort is Essential for Growth 10

    The Cost of Staying Comfortable 11

    Growth in Personal Relationships: Emma's Story 11

    The Role of Discomfort in Building Resilience 12

    Discomfort in Professional Growth: David's Story 14

    The Turning Point: Embracing Discomfort 15

Implementing Accountability Measures 16

The Outcome: Growth, Trust, and Productivity 17

The Science Behind Discomfort and Growth....................18

Practical Steps to Embrace Discomfort......................................19

Reflection Prompts 21

Challenge: Step into Discomfort 23

Sources for Chapter 2...23

Notes Section 24

Chapter 3 The UnTruth of "Nice" Leadership 25

The Problem with "Nice" Leadership 25

What "Nice" Leaders Miss: Accountability and Growth 26

Example: Overcoming "Nice" Leadership: Sarah's Turning Point: Shifting from Avoidance to Accountability 26

The Impact: A Culture of Accountability and Trust 30

Example of the Cost of Niceness in Organizational Culture: Chris' Story: Shifting from "Nice" Leadership to Accountability 31

Facing the Reality: "Nice" Leadership Has a Cost......................32

The Shift: Embracing Accountability with Respect....................32

The Outcome: A Balanced Culture of Kindness and Accountability 33

Building Trust Through Honesty..33

Reflection Prompts 35

Challenge: Embrace Brutal Honesty in Leadership..................... 36

Sources for Chapter 3... 36

Notes Section.. 37

Chapter 4: Embracing Discomfort for Personal and Professional Growth 38

The Growth that Lies Beyond Comfort............................. 38

The Downside of Staying Comfortable 39

Example: Personal Growth through Discomfort: Anna's Story: Confronting Fear to Achieve Career Growth 39

The Role of Discomfort in Developing Resilience 40

Example: Facing Discomfort to Improve Relationships: Liam's Story: Addressing Conflict for Relationship Growth 41

    Facing the Fear of Discomfort 42

    The Difficult Conversation.. 43

    The Positive Transformation.. 44

Practical Strategies for Embracing Discomfort 45

Reflection Prompts.. 47

Challenge: Step Out of Your Comfort Zone............................... 49

Sources for Chapter 4.. 49

Notes Section.. 51

Chapter 5: The Value of Brutal Honesty in Leadership...... 52

The Concept of Brutal Honesty.. 52

Why Brutal Honesty is a Strength in Leadership........................ 53

Example: Transforming a Team Through Brutal Honesty: Jake's Story: Embracing Brutal Honesty in a Failing Team 53

Strategies for Practicing Brutal Honesty in Leadership 55

The Importance of Accountability in a Culture of Brutal Honesty 57

Creating an Accountability System 57

Example: Accountability and Brutal Honesty at the Organizational Level: Alex's Story: Building Accountability in a High-Pressure Environment 58

Reflection Prompts 60

Challenge: Practice Brutal Honesty This Week 62

Sources for Chapter 5 62

Notes Section 63

Chapter 6: The Power of Constructive Feedback in Building a Growth Mindset 64

The Role of Constructive Feedback 64

Why Constructive Feedback is Essential for Growth 65

Example: Turning Feedback into a Tool for Growth: Rachel's Story: Building a Growth Mindset in a Fast-Paced Environment 65

Strategies for Providing Constructive Feedback 67

The Long-Term Benefits of a Growth Mindset Culture . 69

Example: Building a Culture of Feedback: Jordan's Story: Establishing Constructive Feedback as a Core Value 69

Reflection Prompts 72

Challenge: Seek and Give Constructive Feedback 74

Sources for Chapter 6 74

Notes Section 76

Chapter 7: Empathy, Your Leadership Superpower—
Understanding the Perception of Others 77

Why Empathy Matters in Leadership 77

Empathy vs. Sympathy: Understanding the Difference 78

Example: Using Empathy to Navigate Conflict: David's Story:
Resolving Team Tension with Empathy 78

Strategies for Cultivating Empathy in Leadership 80

The Role of Empathy in Decision-Making 82

Example: Empathy-Driven Decision Making: Lila's Story:
Balancing Business Needs with Empathy 82

Reflection Prompts 85

Challenge: Practice Empathy in a Challenging Situation 88

Sources for Chapter 7 88

Notes Section 90

Chapter 8: The Strength of Vulnerability—Leading with
Authenticity 91

Redefining Vulnerability in Leadership 91

The Difference Between Oversharing and Authentic Vulnerability
.... 92

Example: Embracing Vulnerability in a Crisis: Rebecca's Story:

Leading with Openness During a Challenging Transition.........93

Strategies for Leading with Vulnerability............................94

The Benefits of Vulnerability in Team Dynamics.......................96

Example: Using Vulnerability to Empower Others: Carlos's Story: Building a Culture of Trust and Support..........................96

Reflection Prompts 99

Challenge: Embrace Vulnerability in a Key Interaction 101

Sources for Chapter 8 101

Notes Section 103

Chapter 9: The Role of Self-Awareness in Effective Leadership... 104

The Power of Self-Awareness in Leadership............................ 104

Understanding Self-Awareness and Its Two Dimensions 105

Example: The Impact of Self-Awareness on Decision-Making: Tom's Story: Recognizing Blind Spots for Better Leadership 106

Strategies for Building Self-Awareness............................. 107

Example: Using Self-Awareness to Overcome Imposter Syndrome: Emily's Story: Embracing Her Unique Strengths as a Leader 109

The Ripple Effect of Self-Awareness in Teams 110

Reflection Prompts 111

Challenge: Embrace Self-Awareness in a Leadership Situation 113

Sources for Chapter 9 113

Notes Section 115

Chapter 10: Leading with Purpose—Aligning Actions with Values 116

   The Power of Purpose in Leadership 116

   Identifying Your Leadership Purpose 117

   Example: Leading with Purpose to Inspire Change: Anna's Story: Building a Culture of Integrity and Inclusion 118

   Strategies for Leading with Purpose 119

   The Benefits of Purpose-Driven Leadership for Team Dynamics 121

   Example: Inspiring a Team with Purpose: James's Story: Turning a Sales Team into Purpose-Driven Champions 121

   Reflection Prompts 123

   Challenge: Define and Live Your Leadership Purpose 125

   Sources for Chapter 10 125

   Notes Section 127

   Closing Thoughts 128

Dedication

To my family,

Thank you for enduring this journey with me. I cannot fully express how deeply grateful I am for your unwavering love and support as I wrestle with the questions and challenges that life presents. Your patience, understanding, and belief in me have been my anchor as I search for answers to the mysteries that often seem just out of reach.

This book is as much yours as it is mine.

With love and gratitude.

Author's Note

I began this journey because of my own struggles in effectively communicating with the people I care about. If we're lucky, we have family, friends, colleagues, and others whom we truly care for and want to help. But wanting to help and knowing how to do so effectively are two very different things. Many of us struggle with delivering The Truth - not because we don't know it, but because we fear how it will be received. We worry about damaging relationships, about pushing someone further away instead of helping them, about becoming the villain in a story where we only intended to be the guide.

While I have faced this challenge with many people in my life, one person, in particular, weighs on me the most. And I know I'm not alone. I see the echo chamber surrounding them, the people who love them, support them, and want the best for them - yet all of us, myself included, struggle to break through their UnTruths. Fear of rejection? Fear of conflict? Fear of admitting we don't have all the answers either. I don't know. But what I do know is that, in my opinion, this person has been robbed of years of a more prosperous and fulfilling life, not by circumstance, but by the narratives they've chosen to believe.

I admit my own biases here. My own judgments.

Perhaps this is the life they imagined for themselves, and I struggle with my definition of what that should look like. Maybe my desire to challenge their perspective is less about helping them and more about my own discomfort in watching them make choices I cannot understand. And if we could strike up an open, honest conversation about it - without my own fears clouding my words, I might see their reality differently.

But what if their reality is not truly theirs? What if it is one supported and maintained by the UnTruths told to them - by those around them, by the world they consume, and even by their own internal narratives? What if kindness, as they experience it, is simply the comfort of never having to question these UnTruths? And what if my reluctance to push harder, to be more direct, to hold up a mirror to the distortions they've accepted, has contributed to their continued stagnation?

You, the reader, probably already have someone in mind. Someone in your own life for whom this story resonates. A person you care deeply about, whom you've tried to help, only to find yourself struggling to bridge the gap between what you see and what they believe.

My sincere hope is that this journey provides me with the insight to be more effective in helping others grow, thrive, and flourish - and along the way, helps you, the reader, do the same. Together, maybe we can make the world a better place, not by withholding truths in the name of kindness, but by learning how to share them in a way that is both courageous and compassionate.

And to those I have encountered along this journey - those to whom I failed to prove my authenticity and sincerity when sharing my version of the Truth - I apologize. I truly meant it from a place of love. At the time, I believed it was the kindest act I could offer. I am not perfect. I continue to struggle, to grow, and to be better.

This book is not a lecture. It is a challenge. A conversation. An invitation to explore the uncomfortable truths that shape our lives. If we face them together, perhaps we can learn how to communicate not just with kindness, but with clarity, courage, and impact.

Introduction

"Kindness, in the wrong hands, becomes the enemy of truth."

This statement is designed to challenge your assumptions right from the start. It highlights this book's central premise: that what we often call kindness in today's culture can, in fact, be a dangerous form of avoidance. When kindness becomes untruth, it holds people back from their true potential.

The UnTruth of Kindness

The "UnTruth" of kindness refers to the way kindness is often misapplied as a tool to avoid discomfort rather than to foster growth. Kindness, in its most honest form, is not about shielding others from hard truths, it's about supporting them through difficult realities.

However, in our society, kindness has often been twisted into a practice that prioritizes harmony and avoidance over authenticity and courage.

When we choose comfort over truth, we engage in what I call the "UnTruth." This untruth disguises itself as compassion but ultimately stifles real growth. We avoid difficult conversations, soften feedback, and allow complacency to settle in because we believe we're being kind. In reality, this version of kindness is a disservice. It encourages stagnation rather than progress, often leaving people unprepared to face the realities of life.

The UnTruth of Kindness, therefore, is this: when kindness becomes an excuse to avoid discomfort, it no longer serves as a force for good but rather as a barrier to growth. This book invites you to rethink kindness, challenging the assumption that it's kinder to avoid hard truths. True kindness requires us to be honest, even when it's uncomfortable, because it is only through discomfort that real growth and transformation happen.

The True Cost of Avoidance

Avoidance is easy. It's easier to avoid giving direct feedback than to risk an uncomfortable conversation. It's easier to smile and nod, telling someone they're doing fine, rather than acknowledging where they might need improvement. But this avoidance comes with hidden costs.

Leaders, managers, friends, family members, we all encounter moments when honesty could lead to growth, but we choose comfort instead. These moments add up, gradually creating a culture where people prioritize feelings over facts, comfort over growth, and avoidance over truth.

This book aims to dismantle the notion that kindness must always feel good. In fact, some of the kindest actions don't feel good at all. They require us to be brutally honest, to hold others accountable, and to have the courage to say what needs to be said. True kindness is about fostering resilience, pushing people beyond their comfort zones, and supporting them as they grow through discomfort.

Embracing Brutal Honesty

In these pages, we'll explore the power of brutal honesty—not as a weapon, but as a tool for transformation. Brutal honesty is not about harshness or cruelty; it's about clarity and directness. It's about saying what needs to be said, without sugar-coating, because the truth is often what people need most, even when it's uncomfortable.

This kind of honesty doesn't just benefit the individual; it also strengthens teams, families, and organizations. When we foster a culture of honesty, we build trust, enhance accountability, and enable true growth. Through this book, you'll discover how to replace unproductive niceties with productive truth-telling, how to recognize when kindness is becoming avoidance, and how to cultivate resilience through honesty.

Each chapter is designed to guide you through these principles, with examples, Reflection Prompts, and

Challenges to apply what you've read to your own life. Use these exercises to delve into your own experiences, confront your patterns of avoidance, and take steps toward becoming a kinder, more honest, and more impactful version of yourself.

So, are you ready to re-evaluate what it means to be kind? Are you willing to embrace discomfort, to challenge assumptions, and to grow? If so, let's begin this journey together toward a more authentic, honest, and courageous way of living.

Chapter 1
Defining UnTruth

"Untruth is any distortion of reality - whether through avoidance, omission, or sugar-coating - intended to spare discomfort, but ultimately preventing growth and progress."

What is UnTruth?

An untruth is not necessarily a lie; rather, it's a softened version of reality, a conversation carefully framed to avoid offending or hurting someone's feelings. It's the discomfort we bypass when we avoid giving hard feedback or addressing performance issues head-on. We do it under the guise of kindness, but in reality, we are often protecting our own comfort, not truly supporting the growth of others.

In today's world, people in all roles—leaders, friends, family members—find themselves grappling with the idea of avoiding discomfort for kindness's sake. We think that sparing someone the pain of direct feedback is "doing the right thing," but avoiding these hard truths doesn't protect others—it robs them of the opportunity to improve, to develop, and to grow.

This chapter is about peeling back that thin layer of comfort, exposing untruth, and embracing brutal honesty as an act of genuine kindness.

The True Meaning of Brutal Honesty

Brutal honesty is often misunderstood. For many, the word "brutal" brings to mind harshness or cruelty, but here, "brutal" simply means unfiltered. Brutal honesty involves saying what needs to be said, without softening, because the truth, even if uncomfortable, is ultimately kind.

When practiced effectively, brutal honesty is an act of courage and compassion. This honesty might cause temporary discomfort, but it brings clarity, fosters accountability, and creates a foundation for growth. **Without brutal honesty, we live in ambiguity, stagnate, and avoid progress**. This is where UnTruth takes root, often wrapped in the guise of kindness.

The Pitfalls of Avoidance

Avoiding hard truths is common. Many of us rationalize avoidance by telling ourselves we're being considerate, but often, we're simply protecting our own comfort. Addressing difficult topics requires a level of vulnerability, of stepping into discomfort. It's easier to hold back, soften the truth, or ignore it altogether.

However, avoidance comes at a cost. When we avoid addressing reality, we allow problems to grow unchecked. Minor issues can escalate, and unspoken frustrations can turn into resentment. Avoidance, when presented as kindness, ultimately erodes trust and hinders growth.

Consider this: **Is it truly kind to let someone remain unaware of where they can improve?** Is it supportive to allow a person to continue down a path that isn't serving them?

Brutal honesty forces us to ask these difficult questions and to redefine our understanding of kindness.

The Cost of Avoiding the Truth: Rachel's Story

Rachel is the COO of a rapidly growing fitness company. Known for her empathetic approach, she values harmony and tries to avoid difficult conversations, believing it's kinder to shield her team from harsh truths.

Over time, Rachel notices that her approach is causing problems. Team members avoid addressing issues openly, and minor frustrations turn into larger conflicts. When one of her senior managers, Mark, makes a significant error in a major project, Rachel softens her feedback, hoping to avoid hurting his confidence. But this only leads to more mistakes, and the whole team suffers.

Eventually, Rachel realizes that her reluctance to be direct is holding her team back. She decides to hold a meeting, openly acknowledging her own mistakes and committing herself to honesty. By embracing brutal honesty, Rachel fosters a culture where her team feels empowered to face challenges head-on, leading to innovation, growth, and higher morale.

Rachel's story illustrates a truth that many grapple with: **avoiding hard conversations may seem kind, but it ultimately stifles progress and erodes trust.**

Honesty as a Growth Catalyst

Brutal honesty, when practiced effectively, is a catalyst for growth. Research from the **Harvard Business Review** reveals that **70% of employees** who received honest feedback felt more engaged, while those who received only positive feedback tended to plateau in their performance.

Why does brutal honesty work?

- **It eliminates ambiguity** - When we know exactly where we stand, we can take decisive action to improve.

- **It fosters Accountability** - Clarity allows individuals to take ownership of their growth.

- **It creates a culture of trust** – Teams that embrace honest feedback develop resilience and collaboration.

In short, **honesty creates a foundation of trust and accountability**, without which genuine growth cannot occur.

Reflection Prompts

1. Where Have You Avoided the Truth?

Think about areas in your life where you've avoided speaking the truth because it felt uncomfortable. Was it with a colleague, a friend, or a family member? Write down one or two examples where you've softened the truth in the name of kindness.

o Example: "I avoided giving my coworker feedback on their work because I didn't want to hurt their feelings."

_____

_____

_____

2. What Was the Impact of Avoiding the Truth?

For each situation where you avoided discomfort, consider the consequences. Did things improve or worsen over time? How did avoiding the truth impact your relationship with the person involved or your own sense of integrity?

- Example: "Because I didn't speak up, the issue continued, and I grew frustrated, which damaged our working relationship."

_____
_____
_____

3. How Could Honesty Have Changed the Outcome?

Reflect on how the situation might have been different if you had been honest from the start. Could the relationship have improved? Would addressing the issue early have led to growth or resolution sooner?

- Example: "If I had been honest, we could have worked together to fix the problem, and I wouldn't have harbored resentment."

_____
_____
_____

Challenge: Speak an Uncomfortable Truth

Identify one situation in your life where you've been avoiding the truth. Challenge yourself to have an honest conversation with that person or in that setting within the next week.

Write down the situation, the truth you've been avoiding, and what steps you'll take to address it.

- **Situation:** "I need to give my team feedback about missed deadlines."

- **The Uncomfortable Truth:** "The team isn't meeting expectations, and it's affecting our overall performance."

- **Action Step:** "Schedule a meeting to address the issue and provide clear, honest feedback."

Sources for Chapter 1

1. Buckingham, M., C Goodall, A. (2019). *The Feedback Fallacy.* Harvard Business Review. https://hbr.org/2019/03/the-feedback-fallacy.

2. Beck, A. T. (1979). *Cognitive Therapy and the Emotional Disorders.* New York: Penguin.

3. Dalio, R. (2017). *Principles: Life and Work.* New York: Simon C Schuster.

Notes Section

Use this space to jot down any additional thoughts, reflections, or personal insights that came up for you while reading this chapter.

_____
_____
_____
_____
_____
_____
_____
_____
_____
_____
_____
_____
_____
_____
_____
_____
_____
_____
_____

Chapter 2
Growth Through Discomfort

"Growth begins at the edge of your comfort zone."

– Unknown

Why Discomfort is Essential for Growth

Discomfort is a universal experience and a powerful motivator for personal development. It's often viewed as something to be avoided, yet discomfort can serve as a bridge between where we are and where we aspire to be. Every major transformation - whether in leadership, personal growth or professional success – requires stepping into the unknown, confronting challenges, and pushing us beyond our known limits to bring about transformative growth.

Psychologists call this the "stretch zone"—the area where we operate just beyond our comfort zone, encouraging adaptation and growth without overwhelming us. Studies reveal that people who engage in challenging experiences develop greater resilience, adaptability, and confidence. **In contrast, those who remain in their comfort zones tend to stagnate, develop limiting beliefs, and lose motivation over** time.

The Cost of Staying Comfortable

While comfort feels safe, staying in it for too long can lead to unproductive habits, unfulfilling routines, and a sense of unspoken dissatisfaction. Avoiding discomfort holds us back from the opportunities to grow, learn, and evolve. The need for constant comfort is often a hidden barrier to success and true self-development.

Consider workplaces where difficult conversations are often avoided. Over time, unresolved issues accumulate, and this habit of avoiding discomfort can weaken team dynamics, reduce productivity, and create an environment where unresolved issues remain beneath the surface. This fosters a culture where feedback is absent and when managers or team members sidestep difficult conversations, problems are rarely resolved. **By prioritizing comfort over growth**, leaders may unintentionally create environments where complacency thrives, and challenges are never fully addressed.

Growth in Personal Relationships: Emma's Story

Emma is a dedicated, deeply empathetic friend who values harmony and avoids conflict. When her best friend, Sarah, consistently fails to keep commitments,

Emma decides not to mention it, fearing it might damage their friendship, so she convinces herself that it's kinder to remain silent.

Over time, Emma's frustration grows. She begins to resent Sarah's behavior but still avoids addressing it. Finally, one day, after Sarah forgets an important event that they had planned together, Emma finally decides to share her feelings honestly. At first, Sarah is caught off guard, but as they discuss it openly, she realizes and begins to understand the impact her behavior has had. This candid conversation leads to a new level of trust between them. Emma's willingness to embrace discomfort strengthens their friendship and allows both to grow.

Emma's story highlights that **discomfort in relationships isn't something to be feared; it's often a necessary step toward deeper, more authentic connections.** In avoiding these moments, we risk allowing resentment to build and relationships to weaken. Embracing discomfort fosters open communication, trust, and mutual growth.

The Role of Discomfort in Building Resilience

Resilience is built through exposure to challenge and adversity. When we embrace discomfort, we become better equipped to handle setbacks, uncertainty, and adversity. Research on psychological resilience shows that people who actively face challenges head-on tend to report **higher satisfaction, stronger coping skills, and greater adaptability in life – ultimately leading to personal growth in life.**

Discomfort is a powerful teacher. It teaches us:

- How to remain focused under pressure.
- To adapt when circumstances are unpredictable and beyond our control.
- To persist through difficulties to achieve meaningful success.

When we avoid discomfort, we miss these essential lessons.

To illustrate, **consider athletes** who train rigorously to achieve peak performance. Athletes know that their bodies adapt to the demands placed on them, growing stronger with every challenge. Just as athletes strengthen their muscles through physical strain, we strengthen our mental resilience through the challenges we face and overcome.

Discomfort in Professional Growth: David's Story

In professional settings, the ability to embrace discomfort is often what sets top performers apart. **Leaders who are willing to address issues, challenge norms, and step outside of established patterns create environments that encourage innovation and growth**. They push their teams to reach higher standards and adapt to changing demands.

David had been with his software company for over five years, earning a reputation as a considerate and approachable project manager. He took pride in maintaining positive relationships with his team members, but as the company expanded, David found himself overseeing increasingly complex projects with tighter deadlines and higher stakes. His management style, focused on keeping harmony and avoiding conflict, had always worked well with smaller, less demanding teams. However, as project timelines started slipping and deliverables piled up, David's approach was put to the test.

David noticed that several team members were consistently missing deadlines and submitting work that required extensive revisions. Though he sensed that some team members weren't fully engaged, he hesitated to address these performance issues directly. He worried that tough conversations might create tension and undermine team morale.

Instead, he continued to encourage his team in general terms, assuming they would recognize the need to improve on their own.

Over time, however, the situation worsened. Team members started deflecting blame when projects fell behind, and some began voicing frustrations about carrying extra workloads. Morale began to decline, and even David was feeling the impact. Each missed deadline brought him more stress, and he found himself working late to make up for the team's lapses. Eventually, the higher-ups noticed the recurring delays and called David in for a meeting to discuss performance. Feeling the pressure mounting, David realized that his habit of avoiding discomfort was no longer sustainable.

The Turning Point: Embracing Discomfort

After the meeting with senior management, David decided to take a different approach. He acknowledged that his reluctance to provide direct feedback and address issues head-on had allowed the problems to persist. Determined to foster a more accountable and engaged team, he scheduled individual one-on-one meetings with each team member to discuss performance and expectations.

In these meetings, David was open about his own challenges and acknowledged that he had failed to address certain issues early on. He shared that his priority moving forward was to create a more transparent and accountable team environment. With this foundation of honesty, David invited each team member to provide their perspective on the challenges they were facing and any barriers they felt were holding them back.

For some team members, the initial discussions were tense. They weren't accustomed to direct conversations about performance, and a few were defensive. But as David continued, he noticed a gradual shift. Team members started opening up about areas where they needed support, sharing ideas for improvement, and suggesting ways they could collaborate more effectively. **David's willingness to embrace discomfort and communicate openly set the stage for a culture of honesty and accountability.**

Implementing Accountability Measures

Following these discussions, David introduced several accountability measures to help track progress and improve team dynamics. Each team member was assigned specific goals with clear deadlines, and David scheduled weekly check-ins to review progress. He also established a system of shared responsibility, where team members were encouraged to hold each other accountable and offer constructive feedback when necessary.

To foster a supportive environment, David made it clear that feedback would be a two-way street. He encouraged his team to share their thoughts on his management style and areas where he could improve. This invitation not only allowed David to grow as a leader but also empowered his team to take ownership of their roles and actively participate in building a stronger team dynamic.

The Outcome: Growth, Trust, and Productivity

In the months that followed, David noticed significant changes in his team. Productivity increased, deadlines were consistently met, and the quality of work improved. Team members seemed more invested in their projects and collaborated more effectively, often offering each other assistance and advice. The environment of accountability, paired with David's openness to honest feedback, had cultivated a sense of mutual respect and trust.

David's decision to confront his own discomfort and address performance issues directly transformed his team. **By prioritizing accountability over comfort, he helped his team recognize the importance of personal responsibility.** His initial reluctance to engage in tough conversations had led to a culture of complacency, but by embracing the discomfort of direct feedback, he fostered a culture of growth and resilience.

The Science Behind Discomfort and Growth

Studies from the **American Psychological Association (APA)** suggest that **exposing oneself to controlled stressors strengthens long-term resilience**. This concept, known as **hormesis**, describes how manageable amounts of stress enhance mental and physical strength. In essence, **growth requires temporary discomfort.**

Key Findings from research on discomfort and learning:

- **Individuals who engage in new, challenging experiences develop stronger cognitive abilities and problem-solving skills.**

- **Employees who receive constructive feedback – even when it's tough to hear – show greater improvement than those who receive only positive reinforcement.**

- **Entrepreneurs who embrace uncertainty tend to innovate more successfully than those who fear failure.**

Practical Steps to Embrace Discomfort

For those who are unfamiliar with embracing discomfort, starting with small steps can be an effective approach. Here are some methods:

1. **Identify Your Avoidance Patterns**: Take note of areas where you habitually avoid discomfort—whether in relationships, at work, or in personal decisions. Recognizing patterns is the first step toward change.

   Example: *"I avoid speaking up in meetings because I fear sounding unprepared."*

2. **Set Small, Actionable Goals**: Begin with manageable challenges that push you slightly beyond your comfort zone. Over time, incrementally increase the difficulty.

Example: *"Next meeting, I will contribute at least one idea, even if I feel nervous."*

3. **Reflect on Positive Outcomes**: After embracing discomfort, reflect on any benefits or lessons learned. This reinforces the positive aspects of facing challenging situations.

   Example: *"I once dreaded public speaking, but after pushing myself to present, I gained confidence."*

4. **Seek Support**: Discuss your challenges with someone you trust. An outside perspective can help you navigate discomfort with encouragement and accountability.

   Example: *"I'll ask my colleague to hold me accountable for giving feedback instead of avoiding it."*

Reflection Prompts

1. Where Are You Avoiding Discomfort?

Think about areas in your life where comfort may be holding you back. Is there a conversation you've been avoiding? A goal you've postponed?

o Example: "I've been putting off asking for feedback at work because it might be difficult to hear."

_____
_____
_____

2. What Has Been the Cost of Avoiding Discomfort?

Reflect on the impact of choosing comfort over growth. Has it kept you stagnant or limited your opportunities? How has it influenced your personal or professional development?

o Example: "Avoiding feedback has kept me from addressing areas for improvement, potentially limiting my growth."

_____
_____
_____

3. **How Could Embracing Discomfort Change the Outcome?**

   Imagine how things might be different if you were willing to face discomfort head-on. Could you gain new skills, strengthen relationships, or achieve greater fulfillment?

   o Example: "Seeking feedback could help me improve, making me more effective and confident in my role."

   _____
   _____
   _____

4. **How Do You Define Growth in Your Own Life?**

   Consider how discomfort plays a role in your personal growth. What are areas where you would like to push your boundaries?

   _____
   _____
   _____

Challenge: Step into Discomfort

Identify one area in your life where you've been avoiding discomfort. Challenge yourself to take action this week. Write down the situation, what you've been avoiding, and the steps you'll take to address it.

- **Situation**: "I need to address performance issues with a team member."

- **What I've Been Avoiding**: "Having a direct conversation about missed deadlines."

- **Action Step**: "Schedule a one-on-one meeting to discuss the issues and set expectations for improvement."

Sources for Chapter 2

1. American Psychological Association. (2017). "The Science of Resilience." https://www.apa.org/topics/resilience/science.

2. Kashdan, T. B., C Biswas-Diener, R. (2014). *The Upside of Your Dark Side: Why Being Your Whole Self – Not Just Your "Good" Self – Drives Success and Fulfillment.* New York: Penguin Random House.

3. Mischel, W. (2014). *The Marshmallow Test: Mastering Self-*

Control. New York: Little, Brown and Company.

4. Dweck, C. S. (2006). *Mindset: The New Psychology of Success.* New York: Random House.

Notes Section

Use this space to jot down any additional thoughts, reflections, or personal insights that came up for you while reading this chapter.

Chapter 3
The UnTruth of "Nice" Leadership

"A leader who always seeks to be liked risks losing the respect of their team."

– Unknown

The Problem with "Nice" Leadership

"Nice" leadership is often misunderstood. Many leaders believe that prioritizing harmony and avoiding conflict will create a positive work environment. While being supportive and approachable is important, **an overemphasis on being "nice" can ultimately undermine team performance, erode trust, and stall growth.**

Research has shown that when leaders prioritize being "nice" over being honest, they create an environment where difficult conversations are avoided, feedback is withheld, and real issues go unaddressed. While a "nice" leader may believe they're preserving team morale, they are often fostering complacency, enabling poor performance, and stifling accountability.

What "Nice" Leaders Miss: Accountability and Growth

"Nice" leadership often prioritizes short-term harmony over long-term growth and accountability. Leaders who focus on being liked or avoiding confrontation frequently sidestep essential feedback, leaving team members unaware of areas where they could improve. Without this feedback, growth is stunted.

The **Center for Creative Leadership** highlights that **honest, constructive feedback is one of the most significant contributors to employee development**. Avoiding these crucial conversations means missing opportunities for improvement and failing to create a culture of accountability.

Example: Overcoming "Nice" Leadership: Sarah's Turning Point: Shifting from Avoidance to Accountability

After several months of frustration, Sarah, a director of a small marketing team in a rapidly growing company, began to recognize that her reluctance to address Greg's performance directly was affecting the entire team. Missed deadlines were impacting other projects, and she noticed that her other team members were starting to question her leadership. Sarah knew that if she continued avoiding these difficult conversations, she would lose the respect and trust of her team. Determined to change, she decided to approach her leadership style with a new mindset: accountability and transparency, rather than mere harmony.

To implement this change, Sarah took several specific steps:

1. Personal Reflection and Acknowledgment

Sarah started by reflecting on her own leadership approach and acknowledging her fear of conflict. She realized that her desire to be liked and to avoid uncomfortable conversations had led her to make excuses for Greg, rather than hold him accountable. This self-reflection was a powerful first step in helping Sarah reframe her role as a leader—not just a friend, but someone responsible for the team's growth and success.

2. Setting Clear Expectations

Before addressing Greg directly, Sarah decided to establish a new standard for her team. She reviewed the project goals, timelines, and expectations, identifying key areas where clarity was needed. She also outlined specific responsibilities for each team member, including accountability measures, so that everyone was aware of what was expected of each other moving forward.

3. One-on-One Conversation with Greg

Equipped with a clear plan, Sarah scheduled a private meeting with Greg. Instead of her usual vague encouragement, she adopted a direct, supportive approach. She began by acknowledging the positive aspects of his work but quickly moved to address the issues she had been avoiding. Sarah clearly outlined where Greg's performance had fallen short, emphasizing the importance of his role in meeting the team's objectives. She provided concrete examples of missed deadlines and quality concerns, making it clear that these issues could no longer go unaddressed.

This conversation was a turning point for both Sarah and Greg. Initially, Greg seemed surprised by her direct approach, as he was accustomed to Sarah's lenient feedback. However, as Sarah continued, he began to understand the impact of his actions on the team. Sarah also offered support by outlining specific steps Greg could take to improve, such as time management strategies and seeking help when needed. By combining honesty with actionable guidance, Sarah set the foundation for Greg to make meaningful changes.

4. Establishing Regular Check-Ins and Feedback Loops

After the initial conversation, Sarah didn't stop there. She scheduled regular check-ins with Greg to review his progress and offer guidance as needed. These meetings served as a continuous feedback loop, ensuring that Greg remained accountable and that Sarah could address any issues in real time. Over time, these regular check-ins became a tool for strengthening their working relationship, as Greg saw Sarah's commitment to helping him improve rather than simply criticizing him.

5. Encouraging Open Communication Across the Team

Recognizing that the rest of the team had also been affected by her previous approach, Sarah held a team meeting to introduce her new commitment to open, honest communication. She openly admitted that she had avoided certain conversations in the past, which may have led to frustration among team members. By acknowledging her own growth as a leader, Sarah demonstrated vulnerability and transparency, encouraging her team to do the same. This set a new standard for the team's culture, where accountability and honesty were valued alongside respect and kindness.

The Impact: A Culture of Accountability and Trust

Sarah's shift in approach had a transformative effect on her team. Greg responded positively to her guidance, making noticeable improvements in his work and meeting deadlines consistently. The rest of the team, seeing Sarah's commitment to honesty and accountability, became more engaged and motivated. They felt a renewed sense of trust in Sarah's leadership, knowing that she would provide clear feedback and address issues openly rather than letting them fester.

Additionally, the new culture Sarah fostered allowed team members to hold themselves and each other accountable. Rather than waiting for Sarah to address performance issues, team members began offering constructive feedback to one another, creating an environment where everyone felt responsible for the team's success. This culture shift led to improved collaboration, higher quality work, and a stronger sense of camaraderie.

Example of the Cost of Niceness in Organizational Culture: Chris' Story: Shifting from "Nice" Leadership to Accountability

Chris had been the CEO of his well-established company for five years. Known for his supportive, empathetic approach, he believed that a positive, conflict-free environment would drive his team's success. He maintained an open-door policy, frequently checked in with team members, and emphasized the importance of kindness and respect in all interactions. Under Chris's leadership, the company enjoyed strong camaraderie and was recognized as a great place to work.

But as the market became increasingly competitive, Chris noticed troubling patterns within his organization. Projects were falling behind, deadlines were being missed, and quality was beginning to slip. Employees seemed hesitant to address issues directly, choosing instead to avoid confrontation and hope problems would resolve themselves. Chris began to realize that while his "nice" approach had fostered a harmonious atmosphere, it had also created an environment where accountability was lacking, and essential issues were swept under the rug.

Facing the Reality: "Nice" Leadership Has a Cost

When a major client threatened to pull out due to a series of delays, Chris was forced to confront the deeper issues within his company's culture. Through conversations with employees and managers, he learned that **many team members avoided direct feedback** to maintain harmony. Managers, in particular, were reluctant to have difficult conversations, worried they might be seen as harsh or unsupportive.

The Shift: Embracing Accountability with Respect

Determined to create a culture that balanced kindness with accountability, Chris implemented several key initiatives:

- **Monthly Feedback Sessions**: Regular sessions allowed managers and team members to discuss performance, challenges, and improvement areas openly, addressing issues early.

- **Training on Constructive Communication**: Workshops taught managers to deliver feedback in a clear, supportive way.

- **Accountability Metrics and Goals**: Clear metrics and goals made feedback straightforward, not personal.

- **Peer Accountability System**: Team members were encouraged to provide feedback to one another, fostering shared responsibility.

- **Anonymous Feedback Channels**: This allowed team members to voice issues without fear of reprisal.

The Outcome: A Balanced Culture of Kindness and Accountability

In the following months, Chris observed noticeable improvements: deadlines were consistently met, and the quality of work improved. His decision to prioritize accountability while maintaining respect empowered team members to take ownership of their roles, building a growth-oriented culture.

Building Trust Through Honesty

Honest feedback is one of the most effective ways to build trust within a team. Studies show that people are more likely to trust leaders who are direct, transparent, and consistent in their communication. Trust is not built on comfort; it's built on authenticity and clarity.

Psychological safety is also enhanced by honest, clear communication. Leaders who practice brutal honesty show that everyone is accountable, including themselves. This builds a foundation of trust and encourages team members to take ownership of their work.

Reflection Prompts

1. Are You Prioritizing Niceness over Honesty?

   _____
   _____
   _____

2. What Has Been the Impact of Prioritizing Niceness?

   _____
   _____
   _____

3. How Could Honest Feedback Improve Relationships?

   _____
   _____
   _____

4. What would it look like to Balance Kindness and Accountability?

   _____
   _____
   _____

Challenge: Embrace Brutal Honesty in Leadership

Identify one instance where you've prioritized being nice over being honest. Challenge yourself to address this situation with honesty in the coming week.

Sources for Chapter 3

1. Center for Creative Leadership. (2020). "The Role of Feedback in Employee Development."

2. Covey, S. M. R., C Merrill, R. R. (2008). *The Speed of Trust: The One Thing that Changes Everything.*

3. Goleman, D., Boyatzis, R., C McKee, A. (2013). *Primal Leadership: Unleashing the Power of Emotional Intelligence.*

4. Edmondson, A. C. (2018). *The Fearless Organization.*

5. Lencioni, P. (2002). *The Five Dysfunctions of a Team: A Leadership Fable.*

Notes Section

Use this space to jot down any additional thoughts, reflections, or personal insights.

Chapter 4:
Embracing Discomfort for Personal and Professional Growth

"Comfort is the enemy of progress."

– P.T. Barnum

The Growth that Lies Beyond Comfort

Discomfort is often viewed as something to avoid, yet it is precisely where growth begins. Whether in our personal lives, careers, or relationships, the greatest moments of development come when we push past what feels comfortable. Embracing discomfort is a skill that can be cultivated, and those who master it find themselves better equipped to handle challenges, adapt to change, and achieve meaningful success.

Psychologists refer to this as the **"stretch zone"**—an area where we are challenged but not overwhelmed. By regularly engaging in the stretch zone, we build resilience, adaptability, and confidence. Studies show that people who experience and overcome discomfort develop stronger problem-solving abilities and a more flexible mindset, essential skills in today's fast-changing world.

The Downside of Staying Comfortable

Comfort zones feel safe and predictable, but they can quickly lead to stagnation and complacency. When we avoid discomfort, we also avoid opportunities for growth.

Relationships become stagnant, skills remain underdeveloped, and we miss out on the personal and professional development that can only come from facing challenges.

Consider how many people stay in jobs that no longer inspire them, relationships that no longer fulfill them, or habits that no longer serve them—all because it feels easier to stay than to change. **Staying comfortable often comes at the expense of fulfillment, progress, and reaching one's potential.**

Example: Personal Growth through Discomfort: Anna's Story: Confronting Fear to Achieve Career Growth

Anna, a software developer, had been with the same company for over five years. She was good at her job, well-liked by her colleagues, and generally comfortable in her role. However, she started to feel a lingering dissatisfaction, a sense that her career was not progressing as it should. When her manager encouraged her to apply for a leadership position, Anna hesitated, unsure of her ability to lead others.

For weeks, she battled with self-doubt, convincing herself that staying in her current role was safer. She worried about failing, about losing the camaraderie she had with her peers, and about the new responsibilities that would come with a leadership role. Yet, deep down, she knew that if she wanted to grow, she would have to face her fear.

Finally, Anna took a leap of faith and applied for the position. After a challenging interview process, she was promoted. At first, she struggled with the new responsibilities, but over time, she developed confidence, honed her leadership skills, and began to enjoy her work in ways she never had before. **By embracing discomfort, Anna was able to unlock a new level of personal and professional fulfillment.**

Anna's journey highlights a critical truth: **growth requires stepping out of our comfort zones**. Had she stayed comfortable, she would have missed out on the career advancement and self-confidence that came from taking on new challenges.

The Role of Discomfort in Developing Resilience

Resilience—the ability to bounce back from

setbacks—is a skill honed through experiencing and overcoming discomfort. Discomfort teaches us patience, adaptability, and mental toughness. Studies in **resilience psychology** indicate that people who confront their fears and work through difficult experiences become more resilient, with a greater capacity for handling stress. Just as muscles grow stronger through physical resistance, our minds and spirits grow stronger through the challenges we overcome. Discomfort is an opportunity to build resilience, equipping us with the tools to handle future challenges with more ease.

Example: Facing Discomfort to Improve Relationships: Liam's Story: Addressing Conflict for Relationship Growth

Liam had always prided himself on his easygoing nature. As someone who valued harmony, he tended to avoid confrontation, both in his personal relationships and at work. He believed that sidestepping conflict was the best way to maintain peace, and his friends and family often saw him as the "peacemaker." However, his approach of avoiding difficult conversations had begun to create silent tensions in his relationship with his partner, Sofia.

For months, small issues had built up between them—unmet expectations, miscommunications, and small annoyances that Liam ignored in the name of harmony. When Sofia expressed frustration over these recurring issues, Liam would brush it off, thinking he was preventing things from escalating. But as he continued to avoid discussing these matters, the unspoken frustrations grew. Liam sensed that Sofia was beginning to pull away, and he feared that avoiding difficult conversations was having a more damaging effect than he'd intended.

Facing the Fear of Discomfort

Liam reached a turning point one evening when Sofia, visibly upset, asked him why he was so unwilling to address issues in their relationship. She expressed how lonely and disconnected she felt, even though they were together physically. Her words struck a nerve, and for the first time, Liam realized that his avoidance wasn't protecting their relationship—it was slowly unraveling it. He felt an overwhelming sense of fear and discomfort at the thought of addressing these difficult topics but also recognized that he had to face them if he wanted their relationship to grow.

Liam decided to confront his fear of discomfort and have an open, honest conversation with Sofia. He asked her if they could sit down and discuss the issues she had brought up, acknowledging that he had been avoiding these conversations out of fear of conflict. By admitting his own vulnerability, Liam hoped to set the tone for an open and constructive dialogue.

The Difficult Conversation

As the conversation unfolded, Liam found himself struggling to articulate his thoughts. He had spent so long avoiding these topics that he wasn't used to expressing his frustrations and fears. He worried that being honest might hurt Sofia or cause her to become defensive, but he reminded himself that discomfort was necessary for growth. He explained how he often held back his feelings because he didn't want to upset her and that he realized now this approach was doing more harm than good.

Sofia, in turn, shared her own perspective. She explained how his avoidance made her feel dismissed and undervalued, as if her concerns weren't important. For her, honesty—no matter how uncomfortable—was essential for trust and intimacy. The more they talked, the more Liam realized that by avoiding difficult conversations, he had unintentionally created an emotional distance between them. They discussed specific instances where unmet expectations had led to frustration and how addressing these issues earlier could have prevented misunderstandings from growing.

Through this uncomfortable but honest dialogue,

they both gained insights into each other's needs and perspectives. Liam understood that facing discomfort was not about inviting conflict but about creating a foundation of trust and transparency. **He learned that openness and honesty were not threats to harmony but essential ingredients for a resilient and fulfilling relationship.**

The Positive Transformation

Following this conversation, Liam committed himself to being more open and addressing issues as they arose, rather than allowing them to fester. He started practicing open communication, sharing his thoughts and concerns more freely and encouraging Sofia to do the same. While it was challenging initially, each honest conversation strengthened their connection. They learned to navigate disagreements with empathy and respect, creating a new dynamic where both felt heard, valued, and understood.

Over time, Liam saw a transformation not only in their relationship but in himself. Facing his fear of conflict had given him a newfound confidence in his ability to handle difficult situations. He found that his relationships with friends and family members also benefited from this shift, as he began addressing minor issues before they became major sources of tension.

Through this journey, Liam discovered that **discomfort is a necessary step in building strong, trusting relationships**. Avoiding conflict may provide short-term peace, but true harmony and resilience come from the willingness to face and work through difficult truths together. The experience taught him that when we embrace discomfort, we create space for genuine connection, growth, and long-lasting bonds.

Practical Strategies for Embracing Discomfort

Embracing discomfort can feel daunting, but there are ways to approach it gradually. Here are some practical strategies to build comfort with discomfort:

1. **Start Small**: Begin by taking small steps outside your comfort zone. If public speaking scares you, start by speaking up in small meetings. If you want to be more assertive, practice with close friends or family. Over time, incrementally push your boundaries.

2. **Reflect on Past Growth**: Think about a time when you overcame a challenge and grew as a result. Reflecting on past successes can remind you that discomfort often leads to positive outcomes.

3. **Seek Feedback**: Ask trusted friends, family, or colleagues to provide honest feedback about areas

where you could grow. Feedback can be a powerful motivator for stepping into discomfort.

4. **Set Goals with Accountability**: Write down your growth goals and share them with someone you trust. Having accountability can encourage you to keep pushing, even when it feels uncomfortable.

5. **Reframe Discomfort as Growth**: Train yourself to see discomfort as a sign of growth. When you feel uncomfortable, remind yourself that it's a sign you're expanding your capabilities and moving toward your potential.

Reflection Prompts

1. What Areas of Your Life Have You Kept Comfortable?

Think about where comfort might be holding you back. Are there goals, conversations, or opportunities you've avoided?

- Example: "I've stayed in a job I don't enjoy because the thought of changing careers feels too overwhelming."

_____

_____

_____

2. How Has Avoiding Discomfort Impacted Your Growth?

Reflect on what staying comfortable may have cost you in terms of personal or professional development.

- Example: "By avoiding feedback, I haven't addressed areas where I could improve, limiting my career growth."

_____

_____

_____

3. **What Might You Gain from Embracing Discomfort?**

   Consider the potential benefits of facing discomfort. Could it lead to improved relationships, career advancement, or personal satisfaction?

   o   Example: "If I had been willing to pursue leadership roles, I might feel more fulfilled and challenged at work."

   _____
   _____
   _____

4. **What Small Step Could You Take to Embrace Discomfort?**

   Identify a small action you could take this week to step outside your comfort zone.

   o   Example: "I'll schedule a meeting to ask for constructive feedback from my manager."

   _____
   _____
   _____

Challenge: Step Out of Your Comfort Zone

Identify one area in your life where you've been avoiding discomfort. Challenge yourself to take action in that area this week. Write down the situation, what you've been avoiding, and a specific step you'll take to confront it.

- **Situation**: "I want to improve my public speaking skills."

- **What I've Been Avoiding**: "Speaking up in team meetings because I worry I won't be clear or confident."

- **Action Step**: "Volunteer to lead a small segment of our next team meeting to start practicing public speaking."

Sources for Chapter 4

1. American Psychological Association. (2018). "Resilience and Thriving: Stress-Related Growth." https://www.apa.org/helpcenter/resilience.

2. Kashdan, T. B., C Biswas-Diener, R. (2014). *The Upside of Your Dark Side: Why Being Your Whole Self – Not Just Your "Good" Self – Drives Success and Fulfillment.* New York: Penguin Random House.

3. Brown, B. (2015). *Rising Strong.* Spiegel C Grau.

4. Duckworth, A. (2016). *Grit: The Power of Passion and Perseverance.* New York: Scribner.

Notes Section

Use this space to jot down any additional thoughts, reflections, or personal insights that came up for you while reading this chapter.

Chapter 5:
The Value of Brutal Honesty in Leadership

"Honesty is the fastest way to prevent a mistake from turning into a failure."

– James Altucher

The Concept of Brutal Honesty

In leadership, honesty is essential—but brutal honesty takes it one step further. Brutal honesty is the ability to communicate truth without sugar-coating or avoidance, regardless of how uncomfortable it may feel. It's about facing challenges head-on, providing unfiltered feedback, and addressing issues directly, rather than sidestepping them to avoid discomfort.

Brutal honesty doesn't mean being harsh or unkind; rather, it's about respecting others enough to communicate openly and truthfully. Leaders who practice brutal honesty build cultures of transparency, accountability, and resilience, where team members feel empowered to address issues early on and correct course as needed. While it may initially create discomfort, brutal honesty establishes a foundation of trust and respect.

Why Brutal Honesty is a Strength in Leadership

Brutal honesty is often misunderstood as harshness, but in reality, it is one of the most effective tools for fostering growth and building trust. Leaders who embrace brutal honesty cultivate a culture where team members feel valued, knowing they will receive genuine feedback that helps them grow. In the long term, brutal honesty leads to better performance, stronger relationships, and a more resilient organization.

The **Harvard Business Review** has published studies showing that employees who work in environments where feedback is direct, constructive, and frequent tend to perform better and feel more engaged. However, today, many leaders still shy away from providing brutally honest feedback, fearing that it might demotivate their team or create tension. Yet, without brutal honesty, team members often remain unaware of areas where they can improve, leading to stagnation and unaddressed issues.

Example: Transforming a Team Through Brutal Honesty: Jake's Story: Embracing Brutal Honesty in a Failing Team

Jake, a senior project manager at a large tech company, was known for his supportive leadership style. He prided himself on creating a comfortable environment for his team and often went out of his way to avoid conflicts or difficult conversations. However, this approach had begun to show limitations as his team struggled to meet project deadlines and consistently missed key performance indicators. When his manager confronted him about the team's poor performance, Jake realized that his reluctance to give brutally honest feedback was contributing to the team's lack of accountability.

Determined to turn things around, Jake decided to shift his approach. He called a team meeting and, for the first time, openly acknowledged the challenges they were facing. Rather than skirting around issues, he outlined the specific areas where performance had fallen short, sharing feedback with each team member on how their individual contributions (or lack thereof) were impacting the project's success.

Initially, Jake's blunt feedback was met with surprise and discomfort. Team members weren't used to such direct communication, and a few seemed defensive. However, Jake emphasized that his intent was not to criticize but to empower them to address their weaknesses and contribute meaningfully. He encouraged them to see feedback as a tool for growth, not a personal attack.

Over the next few weeks, Jake held one-on-one

meetings with each team member to discuss specific areas for improvement, offering support and resources where needed. His brutal honesty began to shift the team's dynamics, as members became more aware of their roles and took greater responsibility for their actions. Performance started to improve, and the team eventually met their project goals. **Jake's shift to brutal honesty transformed the team from a group of complacent individuals into a cohesive, accountable unit.**

Jake's story illustrates how brutal honesty, when delivered with respect and support, can create a culture of growth and responsibility. **His willingness to embrace discomfort allowed his team to reach its full potential** and restored his credibility as a leader.

Strategies for Practicing Brutal Honesty in Leadership

If brutal honesty is unfamiliar territory, here are some practical ways to incorporate it into your leadership approach:

1. **Establish Trust First**: Brutal honesty is only effective if it's built on a foundation of trust. Make sure your team members feel valued and respected before diving into blunt feedback. Start by cultivating a culture of open communication, so they

know your feedback comes from a place of support, not criticism.

2. **Be Specific and Actionable**: When delivering brutally honest feedback, avoid generalizations. Instead of saying, "Your work needs improvement," specify areas that need attention, such as meeting deadlines, quality of work, or attention to detail. Provide actionable steps for improvement, so team members know how to address the issues.

3. **Encourage Two-Way Feedback**: Brutal honesty shouldn't be a one-way street. Encourage your team members to provide feedback on your leadership as well. This mutual honesty creates a culture of continuous improvement and reinforces that everyone is accountable.

4. **Balance Honesty with Empathy**: Brutal honesty doesn't mean being harsh. Approach difficult conversations with empathy, understanding that feedback can be hard to hear. Express your confidence in your team members' ability to improve and offer support as they work through challenges.

5. **Follow Up and Hold Accountable**: Brutal honesty isn't effective if it's a one-time event. Follow up on the

feedback you've provided to ensure that team members are making progress. Hold them accountable for improvements, and be consistent in addressing any recurring issues.

The Importance of Accountability in a Culture of Brutal Honesty

Accountability is a natural extension of brutal honesty. When leaders embrace brutal honesty, they set a standard that everyone is responsible for their actions and performance. Team members understand that while they will be supported, they will also be held accountable for meeting expectations.

Creating an Accountability System

Leaders who implement brutal honesty should establish a system of accountability. This could include regular performance reviews, check-ins, or measurable goals that track progress over time. By making accountability a routine practice, leaders can prevent issues from being overlooked and encourage consistent improvement across the team.

Accountability also extends to leaders themselves. When leaders hold themselves to the same standards they set for their teams, they build trust and demonstrate integrity. This mutual accountability fosters a culture of respect, where everyone is committed to growth and excellence.

Example: Accountability and Brutal Honesty at the Organizational Level: Alex's Story: Building Accountability in a High-Pressure Environment

Alex, the head of a consulting firm, worked in a high-stakes, results-driven environment. Projects were demanding, timelines were tight, and client expectations were high. In the past, Alex had struggled with turnover, as many employees found the pressure overwhelming. Determined to create a more resilient, accountable culture, Alex introduced brutal honesty as a core value in the company.

At the start of each project, Alex made it a point to set clear, specific goals with each team member. She shared what success looked like, what standards were expected, and, crucially, how each person's role contributed to the project's outcome. She emphasized that while the work was demanding, everyone was capable of meeting these expectations—and that they would be held accountable for doing so.

Throughout the project, Alex provided regular, unfiltered feedback. She didn't wait for performance reviews; instead, she addressed issues as they arose. When a team member's work didn't meet expectations, she communicated this immediately, outlining the specific areas for improvement and offering guidance. Her approach was consistent, so team members knew what to expect and learned to see feedback as an opportunity rather than a reprimand.

By the end of the year, Alex noticed a significant shift. The turnover rate dropped, team morale improved, and the firm's reputation for delivering high-quality work grew. Team members expressed appreciation for the clarity, honesty, and accountability that Alex brought to the organization. Alex's commitment to brutal honesty had created a culture where team members felt both challenged and supported, enabling the firm to thrive even in a high-pressure environment.

Alex's story demonstrates the impact that brutal honesty and accountability can have on organizational culture. By clearly communicating expectations and addressing issues in real-time, she built a resilient team that embraced feedback and excelled under pressure.

Reflection Prompts

1. Where Are You Holding Back on Brutal Honesty?

Think about areas where you may be avoiding difficult conversations. Is it with a team member who needs feedback? A peer who could benefit from guidance?

o   Example: "I avoid addressing missed deadlines because I don't want to appear harsh."

_____
_____
_____

2. What Has Been the Impact of Avoiding Brutal Honesty?

Reflect on the consequences of holding back. Has it allowed issues to persist? Has it created misunderstandings or lowered expectations?

o   Example: "By not addressing quality concerns, the team has become complacent, and standards have slipped."

_____
_____
_____

3. How Could Brutal Honesty Improve Your Leadership?

Consider how embracing brutal honesty might strengthen your relationships, improve performance, or foster trust within your team.

o Example: "Providing direct feedback could help team members grow and take ownership of their roles."

_____
_____
_____

4. What Small Step Could You Take Toward Brutal Honesty?

Identify a small action you could take to introduce more honesty in your leadership.

o Example: "I'll start by providing specific, actionable feedback in our next team meeting."

_____
_____
_____

Challenge: Practice Brutal Honesty This Week

Identify one situation where you've been holding back. Challenge yourself to address it with brutal honesty this week. Write down the situation, the feedback you've been avoiding, and a specific plan to address it.

- **Situation:** "A team member's work hasn't been meeting standards."

- **The Brutal Honesty:** "Their work needs improvement, and it's affecting the entire team's performance."

- **Action Plan:** "Schedule a one-on-one meeting to discuss specific areas for improvement and set clear expectations."

Sources for Chapter 5

1. Harvard Business Review. (2020). "The Power of Honest Feedback."

2. Gallo, A. (2014). *The Harvard Business Review Guide to Managing Conflict.*

3. Kim, K., C Mauborgne, R. (2009). *Blue Ocean Leadership.*

4. Scott, K. (2017). *Radical Candor: Be a Kick-Ass Boss Without Losing Your Humanity.*

Notes Section

Use this space to jot down any additional thoughts, reflections, or personal insights that came up for you while reading this chapter.

_____
_____
_____

_____
_____
_____

_____
_____
_____

_____
_____
_____

_____
_____
_____

_____
_____
_____

Chapter 6:
The Power of Constructive Feedback in Building a Growth Mindset

"Embrace feedback; it's not a judgment, but a compass guiding you to where you need to grow."

— *Unknown*

The Role of Constructive Feedback

Feedback is one of the most powerful tools in a leader's arsenal. When used effectively, constructive feedback can inspire growth, ignite motivation, and drive continuous improvement. However, not all feedback is created equal. Constructive feedback goes beyond simply identifying mistakes; it highlights areas for improvement and provides actionable guidance on how to achieve better results.

The goal of constructive feedback is to foster a **growth mindset**—a belief that abilities can be developed through hard work, learning, and persistence. Leaders who provide constructive feedback create an environment where team members feel encouraged to stretch their abilities, learn from mistakes, and pursue excellence. In contrast, feedback that is vague or overly critical can demotivate and discourage.

Why Constructive Feedback is Essential for Growth

People thrive when they know exactly what they need to improve and have clear steps to get there. Constructive feedback builds this bridge by identifying specific areas for development and encouraging personal responsibility. Studies from **Stanford University** indicate that individuals who receive constructive feedback tend to show higher levels of motivation and engagement, as they see mistakes as opportunities rather than failures.

Constructive feedback also builds trust. Leaders who provide clear, actionable feedback show their team that they are invested in their growth. This helps establish a culture where team members feel valued and supported in their journey of self-improvement.

Example: Turning Feedback into a Tool for Growth: Rachel's Story: Building a Growth Mindset in a Fast-Paced Environment

Rememer Rachel, the COO of a rapidly growing fitness company, she faced a common challenge. As the company expanded, her team had to meet increasingly high standards, and performance expectations were higher than ever. While her team was talented and dedicated, Rachel noticed a trend: team members tended to shy away from tasks where they feared failure, preferring to stick to familiar routines. This reluctance to embrace new challenges was holding the team back from reaching their full potential.

Rachel knew she needed to cultivate a growth mindset within her team, but she also understood that simply telling people to "take risks" wouldn't be enough. She decided to implement a strategy of regular, constructive feedback as a way to encourage her team members to step outside their comfort zones. She began by scheduling one-on-one meetings with each team member to discuss their goals, areas of strength, and areas where they could improve. During these conversations, Rachel made it a point to highlight specific instances where they had shown potential and areas where they could challenge themselves further.

For example, one of her team members, Sam, had a knack for creative problem-solving but often held back in meetings. Rachel pointed this out to Sam, encouraging him to take the lead on brainstorming sessions. She explained that she valued his perspective and believed he had the potential to inspire others. By framing her feedback as an opportunity for growth, Rachel helped Sam see his role differently, empowering him to embrace new challenges.

Over time, Rachel's consistent feedback started to shift the team's mindset. Team members began to see mistakes as learning opportunities, rather than setbacks. **By using constructive feedback to reinforce a growth mindset, Rachel created a team culture where individuals were motivated to take risks, improve their skills, and pursue higher standards of excellence.**

Rachel's story demonstrates how leaders can use feedback to instill a growth mindset. **Constructive feedback not only builds skills but also fosters a culture of continuous improvement**, where team members are eager to push their limits and develop new abilities.

Strategies for Providing Constructive Feedback

Effective feedback doesn't happen by accident. Here are some strategies to help leaders provide feedback that motivates and inspires growth:

1. **Be Specific and Relevant**: Feedback should focus on specific behaviors and outcomes, not vague generalizations. Rather than saying, "You need to communicate better," say, "In our last meeting, I

noticed that key points were missed. Let's work on structuring your presentations to highlight critical information."

2. **Use the "Sandwich" Technique Sparingly**: The feedback sandwich—where constructive criticism is placed between positive remarks—can be effective but should be used selectively. Overuse can make feedback seem insincere. Instead, consider focusing on the value of improvement itself as a positive aspect.

3. **Emphasize Actionable Steps**: Constructive feedback should always provide clear steps for improvement. If someone's report lacked detail, suggest adding specific examples or data points next time.

4. **Encourage Self-Reflection**: Instead of only telling team members what to improve, ask them to reflect on their performance and identify areas they feel could be strengthened. This encourages ownership of their development.

5. **Balance Constructive Feedback with Positive Reinforcement**: While constructive feedback is essential, it's equally important to recognize and reinforce positive behaviors. Balance feedback by acknowledging strengths, so team members feel

supported as well as challenged.

The Long-Term Benefits of a Growth Mindset Culture

A growth mindset isn't just about individual improvement; it's about creating a culture where everyone is committed to learning and growth. Teams with a growth mindset are more adaptable, resilient, and motivated to take on new challenges. When leaders consistently provide constructive feedback, they lay the foundation for a learning-oriented environment where setbacks are seen as stepping stones rather than obstacles.

In a **growth mindset culture**, team members are more willing to experiment, innovate, and take calculated risks. They see feedback as a valuable resource, not a critique, and use it to fuel their journey of continuous improvement.

Example: Building a Culture of Feedback: Jordan's Story: Establishing Constructive Feedback as a Core Value

Jordan, the director of a marketing agency, realized that his team was struggling to keep up with the fast-paced industry. Deadlines were being missed, and the quality of work wasn't meeting client expectations. He recognized that part of the problem was a lack of feedback; team members rarely received direct input on their work, and they had become comfortable with meeting the bare minimum.

Determined to create a culture of continuous improvement, Jordan introduced feedback as a core team value. He started by sharing his vision with the team, explaining that feedback would become a regular part of their workflow. Jordan scheduled bi-weekly feedback sessions, where team members could share their progress, discuss challenges, and receive specific guidance on areas for improvement.

In the beginning, there was some resistance. Team members were not used to receiving feedback so frequently, and a few expressed concerns about feeling micromanaged.

However, Jordan made it clear that the goal of feedback was to help them grow, not to criticize. He encouraged open dialogue, inviting team members to share their thoughts and suggestions on how the feedback sessions could be more effective.

Over time, Jordan noticed a shift in the team's attitude. As they became more comfortable with feedback, they started proactively seeking input from each other, collaborating on projects, and supporting each other's growth. Deadlines were met consistently, and the quality of work improved. **By establishing feedback as a core value, Jordan transformed his team's mindset from one of complacency to one of continuous improvement.**

Jordan's experience shows that **feedback can be a powerful catalyst for change** when it's integrated into a team's values and culture. His commitment to constructive feedback fostered a culture of growth, where team members felt motivated to learn, improve, and push their boundaries.

Reflection Prompts

1. How Comfortable Are You with Receiving Feedback?

Reflect on your attitude toward feedback. Do you welcome it as an opportunity for growth, or do you find it challenging?

o Example: "I tend to feel defensive when I receive feedback, but I realize it's an opportunity to learn."

_____

_____

_____

2. What Feedback Have You Avoided Giving?

Think about instances where you hesitated to give feedback. What held you back, and how might constructive feedback have helped?

o Example: "I avoided giving feedback to a team member about their presentation skills, which could have helped them improve."

_____

_____

_____

3. How Can You Use Feedback to Foster a Growth Mindset in Others?

Consider how you can encourage a growth mindset by providing feedback that motivates others to improve.

- Example: "I can provide feedback that focuses on development rather than mistakes, encouraging my team to see challenges as learning opportunities."

_____
_____
_____

4. What Areas Could You Improve by Seeking Feedback?

Identify areas where you could benefit from feedback, either professionally or personally.

- Example: "I could ask for feedback on my communication skills to ensure I'm connecting effectively with my team."

_____
_____
_____

Challenge: Seek and Give Constructive Feedback

This week, challenge yourself to seek feedback on one area where you'd like to improve. Additionally, provide constructive feedback to a team member or peer, focusing on specific, actionable guidance.

- **Area for Improvement**: "I want to improve my time management skills."

- **Feedback You'll Give**: "I noticed that your report could benefit from more detailed examples. Next time, try adding data to support your points."

- **Action Step**: "Schedule a time to ask my manager for feedback on my current workload and time management."

Sources for Chapter 6

1. Dweck, C. S. (2006). *Mindset: The New Psychology of Success*. New York: Random House.

2. Stone, D., Heen, S., C Patton, B. (2010). *Difficult Conversations: How to Discuss*

What Matters Most. Penguin Books.

3. McKinsey C Company. (2019). "The Importance of Feedback for Personal and

Professional Development."

4. Gallup. (2018). "State of the American Workplace: Employee Engagement Insights." Retrieved from https://www.gallup.com.

Notes Section

Use this space to jot down any additional thoughts, reflections, or personal insights that came up for you while reading this chapter.

Chapter 7: Empathy, Your Leadership Superpower—Understanding the Perception of Others

"Leadership is not about being in charge. It is about taking care of those in your charge."

– Simon Sinek

Why Empathy Matters in Leadership

Empathy is one of the most powerful skills a leader can possess. It is the ability to understand and share the feelings of others, allowing leaders to connect on a deeper level, build trust, and inspire loyalty. Empathy enables leaders to see situations from the perspective of their team members, which in turn fosters a culture of compassion, respect, and open communication.

Research from **the University of Michigan** shows that leaders who demonstrate empathy create stronger, more productive teams, as employees feel valued and understood.

Empathetic leaders are better equipped to manage stress, handle conflict, and support team members through challenges. However, empathy requires intentional practice, as it involves not only listening to others but also setting aside one's own perspective to truly understand their experiences and emotions.

Empathy vs. Sympathy: Understanding the Difference

Empathy and sympathy are often confused, yet they are fundamentally different. **Sympathy** involves feeling sorry for someone's situation, which can create a sense of distance and even condescension. **Empathy**, on the other hand, involves stepping into someone else's shoes to understand their feelings and experiences. While sympathy may lead to passive support, empathy actively engages with the person's perspective, allowing leaders to respond in ways that genuinely address their needs.

Example: Using Empathy to Navigate Conflict: David's Story: Resolving Team Tension with Empathy

David, a manager at a marketing firm, found himself caught in a conflict between two team members, Sarah and Mike, who were clashing over a high-stakes project. Sarah, a detail-oriented designer, was frustrated by Mike's more laid-back approach, which she felt compromised the quality of their work. Mike, on the other hand, felt that

Sarah's meticulousness was causing unnecessary delays, adding pressure to meet their deadlines.

At first, David tried to mediate by suggesting compromises, but neither Sarah nor Mike seemed satisfied. Tensions continued to rise, impacting the entire team's morale. Realizing that he needed a different approach, David decided to practice empathy. Instead of focusing on finding a solution immediately, he held separate one-on-one conversations with Sarah and Mike, encouraging each of them to share their perspectives openly.

During these conversations, David learned that Sarah's attention to detail stemmed from a desire to uphold the company's standards and protect its reputation. Meanwhile, Mike's focus on efficiency was rooted in a genuine concern for meeting deadlines and avoiding burnout. By listening to each team member's concerns without judgment, David gained a deeper understanding of the underlying motivations driving their actions.

In a subsequent team meeting, David used this insight to foster a constructive dialogue between Sarah and Mike. He acknowledged the validity of both perspectives, encouraging them to see each other's approach as complementary rather than conflicting. With David's empathetic guidance, Sarah and Mike were able to reach a compromise, agreeing to set clearer checkpoints to ensure quality without sacrificing speed. **David's use of empathy transformed a divisive conflict into an opportunity for collaboration**, strengthening the team's cohesion and boosting morale.

David's story demonstrates that empathy is not about choosing sides or providing solutions immediately. **Empathy allows leaders to uncover the root causes of conflict** and create an environment where team members feel heard, valued, and understood.

Strategies for Cultivating Empathy in Leadership

Empathy is a skill that can be developed with practice. Here are some strategies to help leaders build empathy within their teams:

1. **Practice Active Listening**: Active listening involves giving your full attention, withholding judgment, and responding thoughtfully. Show interest in what team members are saying by making eye contact, nodding, and asking clarifying questions. This demonstrates respect and signals that you value their perspective.

2. **Ask Open-Ended Questions**: Instead of making assumptions, ask questions that encourage team

members to express their feelings and concerns. Questions like "How do you feel about this project?" or "What challenges are you facing?" can provide valuable insight into their experiences.

3. **Acknowledge and Validate Emotions**: When someone shares their struggles, take a moment to acknowledge their feelings. Phrases like "I can see why you'd feel that way" or "That sounds challenging" help team members feel understood and respected.

4. **Put Yourself in Their Shoes**: Imagine how you would feel in a team member's situation, especially if it involves challenges you haven't personally experienced. Consider the pressures, fears, and motivations that might be influencing their behavior.

5. **Follow Up and Show Support**: Empathy goes beyond the initial conversation. Follow up with team members to show that you're invested in their well-being. If someone expresses concerns about a project, check in later to see how they're managing and offer assistance if needed.

The Role of Empathy in Decision-Making

Empathy is not only valuable for one-on-one interactions but also plays a crucial role in decision-making. Empathetic leaders consider the impact of their decisions on team members and stakeholders, ensuring that choices are fair, inclusive, and supportive of the team's well-being.

For example, an empathetic leader who understands the challenges of a high-pressure project might offer flexible deadlines or additional support to alleviate stress. This approach doesn't mean compromising on standards; rather, it ensures that decisions are made with an awareness of their impact on others.

Example: Empathy-Driven Decision Making: Lila's Story: Balancing Business Needs with Empathy

Lila, a regional manager at a retail chain, was tasked with implementing a new scheduling policy that required employees to work longer shifts. While the policy was designed to improve efficiency and reduce costs, Lila recognized that it could also place additional stress on employees, especially those with family obligations or other commitments.

Instead of implementing the policy without question, Lila decided to meet with her team members to understand their concerns and gauge the potential impact. During these conversations, several employees expressed worry about balancing work with personal responsibilities, and one single mother shared her struggles with childcare arrangements.

Taking this feedback into account, Lila proposed a modified version of the policy to upper management, suggesting that employees with specific needs be allowed some scheduling flexibility. She argued that this adjustment would help retain valuable team members while still meeting business goals. To her relief, management approved her proposal, allowing for the changes.

By considering her team members' needs and advocating on their behalf, **Lila demonstrated empathy-driven decision-making**. The adjusted policy not only helped employees manage their responsibilities but also strengthened loyalty and morale, as team members felt valued and respected.

Lila's story illustrates that empathetic leadership is not about sacrificing business goals but about finding solutions that consider the well-being of team members. **Empathy-driven decision-making leads to better outcomes, as employees are more** engaged and committed to the organization's success.

Reflection Prompts

1. How Do You Show Empathy in Your Leadership?

Think about recent interactions with your team. Did you take time to understand their perspectives, or did you jump to conclusions?

- Example: "I often focus on solutions rather than taking time to listen to my team's feelings and concerns."

_____
_____
_____

2. Where Have You Missed Opportunities to Practice Empathy?

Reflect on instances where you might have overlooked someone's perspective or dismissed their concerns. How might empathy have changed the outcome?

- Example: "I could have taken time to understand why a team member was struggling instead of assuming they weren't committed."

_____

_____

_____

3. How Can Empathy Influence Your Decision-Making?

Consider how empathy could play a role in your choices. Could understanding others' experiences help you make more balanced, inclusive decisions?

- Example: "By considering the impact of my decisions on work-life balance, I can make choices that support my team's well-being."

_____

_____

_____

4. What Steps Can You Take to Build a More Empathetic Team Culture?

Identify actions you can take to encourage empathy within your team, such as open discussions, check-ins, or peer support.

o Example: "I'll start by holding regular check-ins where team members can openly share challenges and successes."

_____

_____

_____

Challenge: Practice Empathy in a Challenging Situation

This week, identify a situation where empathy might lead to a better outcome. Challenge yourself to approach the situation with an open mind, actively listening and validating the other person's experience. Write down the situation, the empathetic approach you'll take, and the outcome you hope to achieve.

- **Situation:** "A team member is struggling to meet deadlines."

- **Empathetic Approach:** "I'll meet with them to understand any challenges they're facing and discuss ways we can support their productivity."

- **Desired Outcome:** "To gain insight into their struggles and create a plan that helps them succeed while feeling supported."

Sources for Chapter 7

1. University of Michigan. (2020). "The Impact of Empathy in Leadership."

2. Sinek, S. (2014). *Leaders Eat Last: Why Some Teams Pull Together and Others Don't.*

3. Harvard Business Review. (2018). "Empathy in the Workplace: A Tool for Effective Leadership."

4. Brown, B. (2012). *Daring Greatly: How the Courage to Be Vulnerable Transforms the Way We Live, Love, Parent, and Lead.*

Notes Section

Use this space to jot down any additional thoughts, reflections, or personal insights that came up for you while reading this chapter.

_____
_____
_____

_____
_____
_____

_____
_____
_____

_____
_____
_____

_____
_____
_____

_____
_____
_____

Chapter 8:
The Strength of Vulnerability—Leading with Authenticity

"Vulnerability is not winning or losing; it's having the courage to show up when you can't control the outcome."

– Brené Brown

Redefining Vulnerability in Leadership

Vulnerability is often misunderstood as a weakness, but in leadership, it is a powerful strength. When leaders are willing to be open about their struggles, uncertainties, or mistakes, they create an environment where honesty and authenticity thrive. Vulnerability in leadership is about showing up as a real person, one who isn't immune to challenges and setbacks. This transparency not only humanizes leaders but also fosters trust and connection, encouraging team members to be open and authentic in return.

In a study by **Harvard Business School**, researchers found that leaders who display vulnerability are perceived as more approachable, relatable, and trustworthy. Vulnerability allows leaders to engage with their team on a deeper level, making it easier to work through difficulties collaboratively and build resilience as a team. **Vulnerability is a demonstration of courage**, as it involves taking risks and embracing the unknown, inspiring others to do the same.

The Difference Between Oversharing and Authentic Vulnerability

It's important to note that vulnerability in leadership is not about sharing everything or being overly emotional. Authentic vulnerability is intentional and purposeful; it's about sharing experiences or insights that will help the team grow, learn, or better understand a situation. Oversharing, on the other hand, can blur boundaries, making team members feel uncomfortable or burdened.

Authentic vulnerability involves sharing selectively, focusing on insights that will create value for the team. It means being transparent about challenges without compromising professionalism, and showing that it's okay to be human while still leading with strength and purpose.

Example: Embracing Vulnerability in a Crisis: Rebecca's Story: Leading with Openness During a Challenging Transition

Rebecca was the newly appointed CEO of a family-owned manufacturing company that had recently been acquired by a larger corporation. Her transition into the role was met with resistance from employees who were concerned about changes to the company's culture and operations. Rumors were circulating, morale was low, and Rebecca felt the pressure to deliver results quickly while gaining her team's trust.

At first, Rebecca considered presenting a confident front, but she quickly realized that her team needed more than a display of authority—they needed reassurance and understanding. She decided to address the concerns head-on. In a company-wide meeting, Rebecca openly acknowledged the challenges they were facing and admitted that there were still uncertainties about the acquisition's impact. She shared her own feelings of pressure to make the transition smooth, showing the team that she was aware of the difficulties they were experiencing.

Rebecca's openness resonated with the team. By being vulnerable, she demonstrated that she was committed to the company's well-being and willing to work alongside them to overcome obstacles. She encouraged employees to share their concerns, promised transparency throughout the transition, and committed to listening and adapting as necessary. **Her vulnerability fostered trust**, creating an atmosphere where employees felt comfortable voicing their thoughts and working together to navigate the changes.

Rebecca's story highlights that vulnerability doesn't mean showing weakness. **Vulnerability in leadership means being courageous enough to face challenges openly and invite others to share in the journey.** Her openness built a foundation of trust, enabling her team to come together and support each other during a difficult period.

Strategies for Leading with Vulnerability

Here are some ways leaders can practice vulnerability while maintaining professionalism and purpose:

1. **Acknowledge Mistakes**: Admitting mistakes or misjudgments is one of the most impactful ways to demonstrate vulnerability. When leaders own their errors, they model accountability and show that it's okay to learn from setbacks.

2. **Ask for Feedback**: Seeking feedback from team members demonstrates humility and a willingness to grow. It shows that you value their perspectives and are open to continuous improvement.

3. **Share Personal Experiences**: When appropriate, share a personal story of a challenge you faced and overcame. Make sure the story is relevant to the team's current situation and offers a lesson or insight that will inspire and encourage them.

4. **Be Transparent About Goals and Challenges**: Let your team know the goals you're working toward and any challenges you're facing. Transparency around goals creates a sense of shared purpose and empowers team members to contribute to overcoming obstacles.

5. **Express Appreciation Openly**: Recognizing others' contributions shows vulnerability because it involves acknowledging that your success is not achieved alone. Publicly expressing gratitude demonstrates respect and appreciation for the team's hard work and support.

The Benefits of Vulnerability in Team Dynamics

When leaders are willing to be vulnerable, they create a ripple effect throughout the organization. **Team members feel encouraged to be authentic, to ask for help when needed, and to acknowledge their own mistakes** without fear of judgment. Vulnerability fosters a culture of collaboration, as team members feel safer sharing ideas, taking risks, and supporting one another in moments of difficulty.

Vulnerability also strengthens team resilience. In times of stress, a team that has experienced open, honest communication is better prepared to navigate challenges. **Team members are more likely to rally together**, supporting each other through difficulties and maintaining morale. Leaders who demonstrate vulnerability inspire loyalty and foster an environment where people feel valued for who they are, rather than just what they achieve.

Example: Using Vulnerability to Empower Others: Carlos's Story: Building a Culture of Trust and Support

Carlos, a regional director in a healthcare organization, was responsible for managing multiple clinics in a high-stress, fast-paced environment. Turnover was high, and he noticed that staff morale was often low due to the demanding nature of the job. Carlos knew that to improve retention and job satisfaction, he needed to create a culture where team members felt valued and supported.

One day, during a meeting with clinic managers, Carlos shared his own experience of burnout early in his career. He talked about the toll it took on his mental health and how he learned to recognize the signs of burnout, ask for help, and make changes to prioritize his well-being. Carlos acknowledged that working in healthcare was challenging, and he wanted his team to know that they weren't alone in feeling overwhelmed.

Carlos's vulnerability resonated deeply with his team. Managers began opening up about their own struggles, sharing the challenges they faced in balancing patient care with administrative demands. This honesty sparked a conversation about ways to reduce stress and support each other better, leading to the development of new policies for flexible scheduling and mental health resources.

By sharing his personal story, **Carlos empowered his team to be open about their needs** and to collaborate on solutions that improved work-life balance and morale. His vulnerability created a safe space for others to express themselves, leading to positive changes that benefited the entire organization.

Carlos's story shows that **vulnerability has the power to inspire and motivate**. When leaders are willing to be real about their own challenges, they empower their teams to do the same, creating a culture of trust, resilience, and support.

Reflection Prompts

1. **How Comfortable Are You with Showing Vulnerability?**

    Reflect on your current approach to vulnerability in leadership. Are there areas where you hold back out of fear of being perceived as weak?

    o Example: "I hesitate to admit when I'm unsure, as I worry it might make me seem less capable."

    _____
    _____
    _____

2. **Where Could Vulnerability Strengthen Your Leadership?**

    Identify situations where showing vulnerability could foster trust and connection with your team.

    o Example: "If I acknowledged when I'm feeling overwhelmed, my team might feel more comfortable sharing their challenges with me."

    _____
    _____
    _____

3. How Has Vulnerability Impacted Your Relationships?

Consider how vulnerability has influenced your personal or professional relationships. Has it strengthened trust, deepened connections, or inspired others to open up?

o   Example: "In the past, when I admitted my mistakes, my team seemed more willing to take accountability as well."

_____

_____

_____

4. What Steps Can You Take to Practice Vulnerability?

Outline one or two actions you could take this week to be more open with your team or peers.

o   Example: "I'll ask for feedback on a recent project to show that I value my team's perspective and am open to improvement."

_____

_____

_____

Challenge: Embrace Vulnerability in a Key Interaction

This week, identify a situation where vulnerability could strengthen your connection with others. Challenge yourself to approach this interaction with openness, whether it's acknowledging a mistake, asking for feedback, or sharing a personal insight. Write down the situation, how you plan to be vulnerable, and the impact you hope it will have.

- **Situation:** "I need to discuss a recent mistake with my team."

- **Approach to Vulnerability:** "I'll openly acknowledge my role in the mistake and ask for input on how we can prevent similar issues in the future."

- **Desired Outcome:** "To build trust and show my team that I'm accountable and willing to learn."

Sources for Chapter 8

1. Brown, B. (2015). *Rising Strong.* Spiegel C Grau.

2. Harvard Business School. (2020). "The Impact of Vulnerability in Leadership."

3. Sinek, S. (2014). *Leaders Eat Last: Why Some Teams Pull Together and Others Don't.*

4. Grant, A. (2013). *Give and Take: A Revolutionary Approach to Success.* Viking.

Notes Section

Use this space to jot down any additional thoughts, reflections, or personal insights that came up for you while reading this chapter.

_____
_____
_____
_____
_____
_____
_____
_____
_____
_____
_____
_____
_____
_____
_____
_____
_____
_____

Chapter 9:
The Role of Self-Awareness in Effective Leadership

"Knowing yourself is the beginning of all wisdom."

– Aristotle

The Power of Self-Awareness in Leadership

Self-awareness is the foundation of effective leadership. It's the ability to understand one's own emotions, motivations, strengths, and weaknesses, and to recognize how these influence interactions and decisions. Leaders with high self-awareness can navigate complex situations more effectively, build stronger relationships, and inspire their teams to follow suit. Self-awareness fosters authenticity, allowing leaders to lead with integrity and purpose, rather than being driven by hidden biases or unchecked impulses.

In a **study by Cornell University**, self-awareness was identified as one of the most crucial factors for effective leadership, as it enables leaders to make informed, intentional choices. Self-aware leaders are not only more attuned to their own emotions but also more perceptive of how their behavior impacts those around them. This level of understanding creates a ripple effect, fostering trust, transparency, and open communication within the team.

Understanding Self-Awareness and Its Two Dimensions

Self-awareness consists of two main dimensions: **internal self-awareness** and **external self-awareness**.

1. **Internal Self-Awareness**: This involves recognizing your own thoughts, feelings, and behaviors. It's about understanding what drives you, your core values, and how your experiences shape your perspective. Internal self-awareness is essential for setting personal and professional goals that align with your authentic self.

2. **External Self-Awareness**: This involves understanding how others perceive you. Leaders with high external self-awareness are open to feedback and actively seek to understand how their actions impact others. This insight allows them to make adjustments that improve team dynamics and strengthen relationships.

Balancing both dimensions is key. Leaders who focus only on internal self-awareness may become overly introspective, while those who emphasize external self-awareness may become too dependent on others' opinions. **Effective leaders cultivate both,** using internal insights to guide their decisions and external feedback to refine their approach.

Example: The Impact of Self-Awareness on Decision-Making: Tom's Story: Recognizing Blind Spots for Better Leadership

Tom was a well-respected director at a consulting firm. Known for his analytical skills and problem-solving abilities, he had consistently led his team to success. However, over time, he noticed that some of his team members seemed hesitant to share their ideas during meetings. Despite his open-door policy, Tom realized that he wasn't getting the input he needed from his team to make well-rounded decisions.

After receiving anonymous feedback from his team, Tom learned that his intense focus on efficiency made him appear unapproachable. Team members felt that he prioritized results over their perspectives, which discouraged them from speaking up. Surprised by this revelation, Tom decided to work on his external self-awareness by actively seeking feedback and adjusting his approach.

Tom started by making a few key changes. He began

each meeting with an open-ended question, encouraging team members to share their thoughts without fear of judgment. He also made an effort to recognize individual contributions publicly, showing appreciation for diverse perspectives. Over time, his team became more engaged, and the quality of their discussions improved. **Tom's journey highlights the importance of balancing internal and external self-awareness to create a supportive, inclusive environment where all voices are heard.**

By recognizing his blind spots and actively working to improve, Tom was able to foster a culture of collaboration and trust within his team. **Self-aware leaders not only understand themselves but also create an environment where others feel valued and empowered**.

Strategies for Building Self-Awareness

Self-awareness is a lifelong journey that requires intentional reflection and a willingness to grow. Here are some strategies to help leaders cultivate self-awareness:

1. **Engage in Regular Self-Reflection**: Set aside time each day or week to reflect on your experiences, emotions, and interactions. Journaling can be a helpful tool for exploring patterns in your thoughts and behavior, enabling you to identify areas for growth.

2. **Seek Honest Feedback**: Feedback is one of the most valuable tools for self-awareness. Ask trusted colleagues, mentors, or team members to provide honest insights into your strengths and areas for improvement. Be open to constructive criticism, and use it as an opportunity to learn.

3. **Practice Mindfulness**: Mindfulness helps you become more attuned to your thoughts and emotions in the present moment. By practicing mindfulness, you can observe your reactions without judgment, gaining a deeper understanding of your responses to various situations.

4. **Set Personal and Professional Goals**: Define clear goals that align with your values and aspirations. Reflect on why these goals matter to you, and use them as a guide to make intentional choices that resonate with your authentic self.

5. **Identify and Challenge Your Biases**: Everyone has biases that can cloud judgment. Take time to examine your assumptions, beliefs, and prejudices, and consider how they might influence your decisions and interactions. By challenging your biases, you can make more objective, balanced choices.

Example: Using Self-Awareness to Overcome Imposter Syndrome: Emily's Story: Embracing Her Unique Strengths as a Leader

Emily, a newly promoted manager in a software development company, often felt like an imposter among her more experienced colleagues. She worried that her lack of technical expertise would be seen as a weakness, and she constantly questioned her ability to lead the team effectively. This self-doubt made her hesitant to speak up in meetings or assert her opinions.

To address her feelings, Emily started working on her self-awareness. She took time to reflect on her strengths and weaknesses, recognizing that while she wasn't the most technical person on the team, she had exceptional interpersonal skills and a talent for motivating others. She realized that her role was not to be the technical expert but to support her team's development, foster collaboration, and provide strategic direction.

With this new perspective, Emily began to embrace her unique strengths. She focused on building strong relationships with her team, listening to their concerns, and encouraging open communication. By accepting her value as a leader, Emily was able to overcome her imposter syndrome and lead with confidence. **Her journey highlights the importance of self-awareness in**

embracing one's strengths and recognizing that every leader has a unique role to play.

Emily's story illustrates that **self-awareness empowers leaders to overcome self-doubt and harness their unique abilities**. By understanding her strengths, Emily was able to lead authentically and build a supportive, motivated team.

The Ripple Effect of Self-Awareness in Teams

When leaders are self-aware, they model a behavior that inspires their team members to cultivate self-awareness as well. A self-aware leader creates a safe space where team members feel comfortable exploring their own strengths, weaknesses, and areas for growth. This openness leads to more meaningful connections, improved collaboration, and a shared commitment to continuous improvement.

In a team led by a self-aware leader, individuals are more likely to engage in self-reflection, seek feedback, and take responsibility for their actions. **Self-awareness becomes a shared value**, creating a culture where everyone is focused on learning, growth, and mutual respect.

Reflection Prompts

1. How Would You Describe Your Leadership Style?

Reflect on how you lead and interact with your team. Are there specific qualities or behaviors that define your approach?

o Example: "I tend to be results-oriented, but I realize this sometimes makes me overlook team dynamics."

_____
_____
_____

2. What Are Your Blind Spots?

Think about areas where you might lack awareness or objectivity. Have you received feedback on certain behaviors that surprised you?

o Example: "I tend to avoid difficult conversations, which sometimes leads to unresolved issues."

_____
_____
_____

3. How Do You Respond to Feedback?

Consider your reactions to feedback, both positive and negative. Do you accept it openly, or do you feel defensive?

o Example: "I often feel defensive when receiving feedback, but I recognize that it's essential for growth."

_____
_____
_____

4. What Steps Can You Take to Improve Your Self-Awareness?

Identify one or two actions you could take this week to deepen your self-awareness.

o Example: "I'll ask a colleague for feedback on my communication style to better understand how I come across."

_____
_____
_____

Challenge: Embrace Self-Awareness in a Leadership Situation

This week, choose a specific leadership situation where you can apply self-awareness. Whether it's during a team meeting, a one-on-one conversation, or a decision-making process, challenge yourself to observe your thoughts, emotions, and reactions. Write down the situation, your observations, and any insights gained.

- **Situation**: "I'm leading a team meeting where we'll discuss a recent setback."

- **Self-Awareness Observations**: "I notice that I feel defensive about the setback, but I'll focus on being open and receptive to my team's input."

- **Insights Gained**: "By acknowledging my defensiveness, I was able to approach the discussion more objectively and create a supportive environment."

Sources for Chapter 9

1. Cornell University. (2020). "The Role of Self-Awareness in Leadership Effectiveness."

2. Tasha Eurich. (2017). *Insight: Why We're Not as Self-Aware as We Think, and How Seeing Ourselves Clearly*

Helps Us Succeed at Work and in Life.

3. Goleman, D. (1995). *Emotional Intelligence: Why It Can Matter More Than IQ*. Bantam Books.

4. Harvard Business Review. (2018). "The Benefits of Self-Awareness in Leadership."

Notes Section

Use this space to jot down any additional thoughts, reflections, or personal insights that came up for you while reading this chapter.

Chapter 10:
Leading with Purpose—Aligning Actions with Values

"Efforts and courage are not enough without purpose and direction."

– John F. Kennedy

The Power of Purpose in Leadership

Purpose is the guiding force that drives a leader's decisions, actions, and vision. When leaders understand and embrace their purpose, they lead with a sense of conviction and clarity that inspires those around them. Purpose provides direction, helping leaders to stay focused on what truly matters and make choices aligned with their values. A leader with a strong sense of purpose is resilient, grounded, and motivated to pursue meaningful goals, even in the face of challenges.

Research from **Stanford University's Graduate School of Business** has shown that leaders who are purpose-driven have a higher level of job satisfaction, influence, and long-term success. Purpose-driven leadership not only benefits the individual but also has a positive impact on team morale, engagement, and overall organizational performance. **When leaders lead with purpose, they create a ripple effect that inspires others to find and pursue their own sense of purpose.**

Identifying Your Leadership Purpose

Identifying one's leadership purpose requires introspection and a deep understanding of personal values and motivations. Purpose is not defined by a job title, a set of goals, or external recognition. Rather, it is an inner sense of what truly matters and what one hopes to achieve or contribute to the world. For some, purpose may be rooted in helping others reach their potential, while for others, it may be about driving innovation, creating positive change, or building a legacy.

To uncover your leadership purpose, reflect on these questions:

- What motivates you beyond financial or professional success?

- What impact do you want to have on your team, organization, or community?

- Which values guide your decisions and actions?

- What do you want to be remembered for as a leader?

Purpose is dynamic and may evolve over time. Leaders who revisit and refine their purpose are better equipped to adapt to change, make intentional choices, and lead with authenticity.

Example: Leading with Purpose to Inspire Change: Anna's Story: Building a Culture of Integrity and Inclusion

Anna, the Chief Human Resources Officer at a multinational company, was known for her commitment to fostering an inclusive, ethical work environment. Early in her career, Anna experienced firsthand the negative impact of a toxic work culture where unethical behavior was ignored in favor of financial gain. That experience had a profound effect on her, shaping her belief that **integrity and inclusion must be at the heart of any successful organization.**

When Anna joined her current company, she discovered that there were significant gaps in diversity and ethics policies. She was determined to create a culture aligned with her purpose of integrity and inclusion, even though it meant challenging the status quo. Anna began by engaging with employees at all levels, listening to their experiences, and identifying areas where the company could improve.

She implemented training programs on unconscious bias, established clear guidelines for ethical behavior, and created a diversity and inclusion council to ensure that these values were woven into the company's policies and practices. Though the process required time and effort, Anna's purpose-driven leadership inspired her team to embrace these changes wholeheartedly. **Anna's story highlights the power of purpose in driving meaningful change** and creating a lasting impact on organizational culture.

Through her work, Anna transformed the company's culture into one where integrity and inclusion became core values, improving employee satisfaction, retention, and trust. Her purpose-driven leadership had a lasting impact, proving that **leading with purpose is about creating positive, lasting change that aligns with one's values**.

Strategies for Leading with Purpose

Leading with purpose requires self-awareness, intentionality, and a commitment to aligning actions with values. Here are some strategies to help leaders stay connected to their purpose and lead with greater impact:

1. **Define Your Core Values**: Identify the values that matter most to you. Values such as integrity, respect,

innovation, or compassion serve as a foundation for purposeful leadership. Keep these values at the forefront of your decisions and interactions.

2. **Create a Vision Statement**: Craft a personal vision statement that reflects your purpose and aspirations. This statement can serve as a reminder of your goals and guide you during difficult decisions.

3. **Set Purpose-Driven Goals**: Align your goals with your purpose. Ensure that each goal reflects your values and contributes to a larger vision. Purpose-driven goals provide a sense of fulfillment and motivate you to pursue meaningful outcomes.

4. **Communicate Your Purpose to Your Team**: Share your purpose with your team and explain why it matters to you. By being transparent about your motivations, you encourage others to connect with their own sense of purpose and support the team's shared mission.

5. **Reflect and Reassess Regularly**: Purpose is not static. Regularly reflect on your purpose, reassessing and refining it as you grow. Purpose-driven leaders are flexible, adapting their purpose as they gain new insights and experiences.

The Benefits of Purpose-Driven Leadership for Team Dynamics

Purpose-driven leadership not only benefits the leader but also creates a positive, engaged, and motivated team environment. Leaders who lead with purpose inspire loyalty and commitment, as team members feel they are part of something meaningful. Purpose-driven teams are more resilient, collaborative, and innovative, as they are united by a shared mission that goes beyond immediate tasks.

In purpose-driven environments, individuals feel a greater sense of fulfillment and belonging. They are more likely to take initiative, support each other, and pursue continuous improvement. Leaders who lead with purpose foster a culture where everyone is encouraged to grow, contribute, and make a difference.

Example: Inspiring a Team with Purpose: James's Story: Turning a Sales Team into Purpose-Driven Champions

James was the head of a regional sales team for a software company. His team was consistently meeting targets, but he sensed that they lacked a deeper motivation beyond hitting numbers. James wanted his team to feel more connected to the company's mission and to understand the value of their work beyond sales quotas.

To inspire his team, James shared his personal story of why he joined the company and how he believed their software could genuinely improve clients' lives. He encouraged his team to see each client interaction as an opportunity to make a positive impact rather than just close a deal. James redefined their success metrics to include customer satisfaction and long-term client relationships, aligning their targets with a purpose-driven approach.

As his team embraced this new perspective, their motivation shifted. They became more invested in understanding clients' needs, providing exceptional service, and building meaningful relationships. **By leading with purpose, James transformed his team into advocates for the company's mission** who were committed not only to meeting targets but to making a difference.

James's story shows that purpose-driven leadership can inspire teams to pursue excellence, not just for immediate rewards but for the greater good. **When leaders infuse purpose into their work, they elevate the impact of their entire team.**

Reflection Prompts

1. What is Your Leadership Purpose?

Reflect on what motivates you as a leader. What impact do you want to have on your team, organization, or community?

- Example: "I want to create an environment where everyone feels valued and supported."

_____
_____
_____

2. How Do Your Values Influence Your Decisions?

Consider how your core values guide your choices and actions. Are there areas where you could align more closely with your values?

- Example: "I value transparency, but I realize I sometimes hold back information to avoid difficult conversations."

_____
_____
_____

3. **What Legacy Do You Want to Leave as a Leader?**

   Think about the long-term impact you hope to have. How do you want to be remembered by your team and peers?

   o Example: "I want to be remembered as a leader who empowered others to reach their potential and fostered a culture of trust."

   _____
   _____
   _____

4. **What Actions Could You Take to Lead with Greater Purpose?**

   Identify specific actions you could take to align more closely with your purpose and inspire others.

   o Example: "I'll start by sharing my leadership purpose with my team and encourage them to explore their own."

   _____
   _____
   _____

Challenge: Define and Live Your Leadership Purpose

This week, take time to reflect on and define your leadership purpose. Write down your purpose statement and identify one action you can take to bring this purpose to life. Share your purpose with a colleague, mentor, or team member for added accountability.

- **Leadership Purpose**: "To create a supportive environment where my team can thrive and grow."

- **Action Step**: "Organize a team meeting to discuss our shared mission, and invite everyone to reflect on their own purpose."

- **Accountability Partner**: "I'll share my purpose with my mentor and ask for feedback."

Sources for Chapter 10

1. Stanford Graduate School of Business. (2019). "The Importance of Purpose in Leadership."

2. Pink, D. H. (2009). *Drive: The Surprising Truth About What Motivates Us.* Riverhead Books.

3. Collins, J. (2001). *Good to Great: Why Some Companies Make the Leap…and Others Don't.*

4. Covey, S. R. (2004). *The 8th Habit: From Effectiveness to Greatness.* Free Press.

Notes Section

Use this space to jot down any additional thoughts, reflections, or personal insights that came up for you while reading this chapter.

Closing Thoughts

Writing, for me, is like holding a mirror up to my own mind—a way to gauge my thoughts and challenge my beliefs. It's my way of thinking out loud in an attempt to make sense of a world that often feels irrational. Through the act of writing, I confront my own perceptions, biases, and assumptions, and in doing so, I find clarity and a deeper understanding. I'll admit, I write better than I speak, though improving communication is a lifelong pursuit for all of us. Writing allows me to connect with readers like you, sharing ideas in ways that verbal expression sometimes can't convey.

Throughout this journey, I've come to accept that no matter how much I study or accumulate knowledge, there is no perfect answer. Growth and improvement will always be accompanied by struggle and discomfort. As we strive to better ourselves, we encounter logical fallacies, errors in judgment, and fragments of misinformation that must be sifted through carefully. Yet, it's in this continuous quest—this honest confrontation with imperfection—that real growth happens.

Every day, I'm profoundly grateful for my life and for the experiences that have shaped me. I am thankful for the relationships I've built along the way, for the people who have taught me, and for those I may have helped in return.

Writing these words is my way of reaching out to you, the reader, in the hope that something here might help you make a positive impact—in your own life, and perhaps, in the lives of those around you. I believe in the power of the butterfly effect, where even the smallest shift can ripple outward, causing profound change and helping others to thrive and flourish.

In *The UnTruth of Kindness*, we've explored how avoiding discomfort in the name of kindness can prevent growth. But the journey doesn't end here. In my upcoming book, *Perception vs Intention*, I'll take this exploration a step further. We'll dive into the gap between how we perceive others' actions and their true intentions—a gap that often leads to misunderstandings, biases, and miscommunication. This next book will build on the themes we've touched on, inviting you to question assumptions, consider others' perspectives, and engage more deeply with the people in your life.

If you'd like to continue this journey, I invite you to visit my website, where you can access early ordering options for *Perception vs Intention* and additional resources that may support your growth. My hope is that together, through these reflections, we can challenge ourselves to grow, communicate better, and make a positive impact in our world.

Thank you for allowing me to be a part of your journey. I'm honored to share these thoughts with you, and I look forward to our continued exploration in *Perception vs Intention*.

www.ingramcontent.com/pod-product-compliance
Lightning Source LLC
Chambersburg PA
CBHW060400080526
44583CB00012B/399